The Chaperon Workbook

Matthew L. Ferrara, Ph.D.

The Chaperon Workbook

Copyright © 2017
Matthew L. Ferrara, Ph.D.

For information about other products created by this author, please visit Amazon Books and search for books by "*Matthew L. Ferrara, Ph.D.*" Or you may contact the author directly at 2500 West William Cannon, Suite 703, Austin, TX 78745. Telephone: 512-708-0502 Fax: 512-708-0557

Email: mferraraphd@outlook.com

CONTENTS

Workbooks by Matthew L. Ferrara, Ph.D. Available on Amazon.com

Workbooks for Adults Who Use Harmful or Abusive Sexual Behavior

1. Ferrara, M. L. (2024) Pathways Program Implementation Guide: How to Use the Pathways, Good Life, and Chaperon Workbooks. F. Free Press

2. Ferrara, M.L. (2024) *Pathways to Healthy Sexuality Second Edition: Treatment for Sexually Abusive Adults*. Kindle Direct Publishing

3. Ferrara, M. L. (2023), *THE Sex Addiction Workbook*, Kindle Direct Publishing

4. Ferrara, M.L. (2014) *The Chaperon Workbook*. Kindle Direct Publishing

5. Ferrara, M. L. (2012) *LEAD Workbook: Treatment for High-Risk Sexual Misconduct*. Kindle Direct Publishing

6. Ferrara, M.L. and McDonald, S. (1996) *Treatment of the Juvenile Sex Offender: Neurological and Psychiatric Impairments*. Jason Aronson, Inc.

Workbooks in Positive Psychology

7. Ferrara, M.L. (2022) *The Good Life Second Edition*. Kindle Direct Publishing

8. Ferrara, M.L. (2022) *All About...Your Emotions!* Kindle Direct Publishing

9. Ferrara, M.L. (2022) *All About...Your Thinking!* Kindle Direct Publishing

10. Ferrara, M.L. (2022) *All About...Your Relationships!* Kindle Direct Publishing

11. Ferrara, M.L. (2022) *All About...Your Self-Management!* Kindle Direct Publishing

12. Ferrara, M.L. (2013) *The Good Life: Principles for Honorable Relationships*. Kindle Direct Publishing

Workbooks in Spanish

13. Ferrara, M. L. (2016) *Limita & Dirige: Manualde Estudiante*. Kindle Direct Publishing

14. Ferrara, M. L. (2022) *Todos Sobre Tus...Emociones: Un libro de la series Good Life*. Kindle Direct Publishing

Workbooks for the Rehabilitation of Juvenile Offenders

15. Ferrara, M. L. (2014) *Limit and Lead Student Workbook.* Kindle Direct Publishing

16. Ferrara, M.L. (1992) *Group Counseling for Juvenile Delinquents: The Limit and Lead Approach.* Sage Publications, Inc.

Behavior Management Training for Staff Working in Juvenile Facilities

17. Ferrara, M.L. (2014) *Training for Trainers Manual: Limit and Lead Behavior Management Program.* Kindle Direct Publishing

18. Ferrara, M.L. (2014) *Direct Care and Security Staff Trainee Handout: Limit and Lead Behavior Management Training Program.* Kindle Direct Publishing

19. Ferrara, M.L. (2014) *Direct Care and Security Staff Trainer's Manual: Limit and Lead Behavior Management Program.* Kindle Direct Publishing

Substance Abuse Treatment Workbook

20. Ferrara, M.L. (1992) *Substance Abuse Treatment Program for Persons with Mental Retardation.* Texas Commission on Alcohol and Drug Abuse.

Sex Offender Treatment Programs That Dr. Ferrara Created or Participated in Creating

Adult	Juvenile	Special Needs
Texas Department of Criminal Justice - Institutional Division	Texas Youth Commission	San Marcos Treatment Center Psychiatric and Neurologically Impaired Clients
Texas Sexually Violent Predator Program	Arizona Department of Juvenile Corrections	
Travis County Community Supervision and Corrections Dept	Youth Development Institute, Phoenix Arizona	

INTRODUCTION

This workbook is written for the person who wants to become a chaperon for an adult with a sexual behavior problem. If you are that person, if you are the one who wants to become a chaperon, you deserve a pat on the back. You are going to take on an important job. It will not be an easy job. Because of your willingness to help, you deserve praise.

In the following lessons, you will learn a lot about sexual misconduct. There are two sections to this workbook. In Section One: Chaperon Training Lessons, you will receive the information necessary to serve as a chaperon. In Section Two: Assignments of Use in Monitoring the Chaperon Contract, you will find lessons to complete once you begin your role as chaperon and are chaperoning someone.

Sex is usually a private thing that is not discussed in public. So, a lot of care was taken to make sure that during this training, you don't have to listen to or talk about any unnecessary sexual topics. When we discuss sex, we discuss only those things that we must discuss. We discuss these things because that is what it takes to become a chaperon. You don't have to worry about being asked about your sexual behavior or desires. If anyone talks about sex, it will be the individual who you will be chaperoning.

The lessons you will go through were written after a lot of chaperons have already been trained. These lessons are based on experience with these other chaperones, so you can be sure that the lessons will address a lot of your questions. Hopefully, you will have a better understanding of the person you are chaperoning and sexual misconduct. Even though these lessons answer a lot of questions, the lessons might not answer all of the questions that you have. Don't be afraid to ask questions; it can only help you and the person you are chaperoning.

Finally, you need to know that you have a choice. At any time during the training, you can choose to stop the training. You don't have to be the chaperon. Or, if you do become a chaperon, you can choose to stop being a chaperon or take a break from being a chaperon. You don't have to do anything you don't want to do. You don't have to listen to any lessons that you don't want to listen to.

Once again, thank you for your courage and the work you are about to do!

SECTION ONE: CHAPERON TRAINING LESSONS

What is a Chaperon?

A chaperon is a <u>companion</u> to someone in treatment for a sexual behavior problem. A good chaperon does the following things to help the person you will chaperon succeed in treatment.

Accompany: The chaperon accompanies the person to different places. Most people in treatment for a sexual behavior problem cannot go to high-risk places. A high-risk place is a place that makes it easy for the individual to use problematic sexual behavior. For example, if an individual's sexual behavior problem is having affairs while alone on business trips, when this individual begins treatment, he or she would not be allowed to go on business trips alone. As the person progresses in treatment, he or she will be allowed to go to some high-risk places, with a chaperon. By the end of treatment, the person being chaperoned and the treatment provider can decide if the individual would be permitted to go to these places without a chaperon.

On occasion, an individual's sexual behavior has gotten them into trouble with the law, e.g., family, criminal, or Child Protective Services court. If the individual you will be chaperoning is involved in the legal system because of his or her sexual behavior, it will be necessary to get permission from the supervising authority before the individual you are chaperoning is permitted to resume going to certain high-risk situations.

Support: The individual in treatment for a sexual behavior problem has to follow many rules. These rules are designed to limit temptation, namely, the individual's access to high-risk persons, places, and things. This can be frustrating for the individual, especially when the rules are in direct conflict with the past habits that got them into trouble. The chaperon can provide support and encouragement to the individual and remind them of the wisdom of following the rules.

At other times, the individual being chaperoned may just need someone to talk to who won't judge them. They may also want someone who can provide good advice and a healthier perspective on a situation. Support especially comes into play when individuals want to talk rather than act on an urge.

Communicate: Since the individual you will be chaperoning is involved in treatment for a sexual behavior problem, you will be required to communicate with the treatment provider. It is crucial that you communicate honestly with the treatment provider about how the individual you are chaperoning is doing with regard to following treatment rules and guidelines. Being "discreet" or trying to protect or cover for the individual you are chaperoning will not help them and may hurt them.

What A Chaperon Is Not…

A dedicated chaperon wants the best for the individual they are chaperoning. That is why a chaperon is usually a trusted friend or a loving family member. To fully understand what a chaperon is, it might be helpful to also know what a chaperon is not.

- **Police:** A chaperon is not a police officer. The chaperon does not go on patrol to make sure the person being chaperoned does the right thing. It is up to the individual to do the right thing.

- **Enforcer:** A chaperon doesn't enforce the treatment rules that a person with behavior problems must follow. It is up to the individual to follow the rules. Chaperons support and encourage, but don't enforce.

Since you care for the individual, you will be chaperoning, you are probably already doing the first two duties of a chaperon: accompany and support. If you want to be a helpful chaperon, you have to add the third duty: communicate.

As a chaperon, you must communicate honestly with the treatment provider. This might be the most difficult part of being a chaperon. The first two duties of being a chaperon, accompany and support, come naturally. Talking with a treatment provider is probably something new and you may find it difficult to do.

Don't make the job of communicating with the treatment provider more difficult than it is. These professionals are ordinary people, who are just trying to help the individual you care about. The more open and honest you are with the treatment provider, the more they can help the individual you care for.

Assessment: Know Your Role

1. Are you a good companion to the person you will be chaperoning? Use the definition of companion in this lesson to answer this question.

2. How different is the role of the chaperon from your current relationship with the individual?

3. Do you feel comfortable communicating with the individual's treatment provider?

4. What is the difference between the role of a chaperon and role of an enforcer or police officer?

5. If you become a chaperon for the individual, how will that help him or her?

How to Respond to Someone with Sexual Behavior Problems

It can be confusing when someone you care about does something wrong or has desires to do something wrong. It can be *really* confusing and disturbing when this individual's problem area is sexual.

Ineffective Responses

If you are like most people, you are pulled between the extremes of denial and distance. While common, these responses will not help the person you are chaperoning.

- **Denial:** If you are in denial, you want to pretend that the person you care about does not have problems related to sexual behavior. If you can't deny that the problem, you deny that it is this person's fault that they have this problem. You blame other people or some external factor. In the case of pornography, you might even say it is a victimless crime.

- **Distance:** Sexual behavior problems are sometimes shocking and may even be repulsive to you, so you may want to distance yourself from the individual with a sexual behavior problem.

If you are in denial or you use distance, you cannot help a person in treatment for a sexual behavior problem. Both reactions are normal and understandable but if you are going to become a chaperon, you must overcome them.

Effective Responses

So, what is the best way to respond?

- **Care about the Person:** If you care about someone, you accept the person as they are. You accept the good with the bad. You can look at the good things they have done…and may still be doing…and feel proud to know them. You can acknowledge the bad things they have done and still maintain your relationship with them. You don't have to pretend the bad things don't exist. Take an honest look at what they did through caring eyes. Use your care and concern to help them, and yourself, overcome their sexual behavior problem.

- **Disapprove of the Behavior, Not the Person**: Even though you care about someone, you don't have to love everything the person has done. Recognize that a person is not simply a sum of their actions. The person you care about who is now in treatment for a sexual behavior problem has a problem that might be difficult for you to accept. Even so, he or she is still the same person who you always cared about. You can accept the person, disapprove of the behavior, and still have a relationship with him or her.

Recognize That Everyone Has Challenges: How much can a problem in one area change a person? Let's see. Imagine that one day you are at the grocery store. You go to the checkout line with a full cart. Another person gets there about the same time that you do. You decide to let the person go ahead of you. You feel pretty good about your choice to be kind.

Now, pretend it is a different day and the same thing happens, except this time you are in a hurry. So, you speed up and push your cart ahead of the other person. Does that make you a bad person? No. It makes you human.

You make different choices on different days. This is the same with the individual you will be chaperoning; a single choice or problem does not define the person.

Face it honestly. Deal with it courageously. Overcome it successfully.

Assessment: How Do You Respond?

1. If I deny that the sexual behavior problem exists, how does that hurt the individual I am trying to help?

2. What do I need to change to make sure that I am not in denial?

3. If I distance myself from the person I am trying to help, how does that hurt my chances of helping him or her?

4. What do I need to change to make sure that I don't distance myself from the person I'm trying to help?

5. How can I care about the person but disapprove of his or her behavior?

Address Your Emotional Response

How did you feel when you learned that the one you will chaperon had a sexual behavior problem? Among the many confusing feelings, you may have been hurt in some way. If you are like many of the chaperons who have trained before you, you may have been hurt in many different ways.

For example, when you learned about the inappropriate sexual behavior, you may have felt embarrassed for yourself or sad for the person with the sexual behavior problem. Even worse, if you know the person who was the target of the sexual behavior problem, you may have felt angry.

All of these reactions are honest, normal, and 100 percent okay.

Whatever your response was, you have to deal with it…or them. But how? There are three general ways that someone may respond to this situation:

- **Grudge:** A grudge is a continuing resentment or desire to see someone hurt because they hurt you. A grudge starts with anger and, as the days, weeks, months and even years roll past, anger snowballs into hate. It becomes an emotional burden that is chained to you and weighs you down wherever you go. It does little to help you or the other person.

  If you hold a grudge against the individual, you will be chaperoning, it may make them feel hopeless, "*Why bother with treatment or following all these rules. It won't do any good anyway. Everyone hates me.*"

- **Pardon:** When you pardon someone, you wipe the slate clean. It's as if the problem never existed. This fantasy may help you, and even the individual you will be chaperoning, feel better ever so briefly. But the problem won't just go away.

  If you pardon the individual you will be chaperoning, it provides them with an excuse to violate treatment rules and guidelines. The individual you pardon may say, "*I don't have to follow the treatment rules. All has been forgiven.*"

- **Forgive**: When you forgive, you acknowledge that the sexual behavior problem hurt you. Then, you inspect your feelings and find a way to stop the pain. Once you have done that, you will be able to be an effective chaperon.

  By forgiving, you say to the person you are chaperoning, *"I know you have a problem and it is not healthy. I will not forget your problem. I will remember it so that I can help you deal with your sexual behavior problem. I still care about you."*

  When the one you are chaperoning hears you say this, he or she will think, *"I don't have to hide anymore. I can finally come clean and get all of this off my chest. I can get the help I need and I will still be connected with my family and friends."*

The way that you respond to the individual you will be chaperoning can either help or hinder them in reaching the goal of **No New Victims!**

Assignment: Forgiveness Statement

You may think that you have forgiven the one you will be chaperoning but don't be surprised if you find that you still hold a little bit of a grudge or you still have the urge to pardon them. It's normal and natural to feel that way, even if it is not healthy. To see how well you can forgive, fill out this *Forgiveness Statement*. Be prepared to discuss your thoughts and feelings with the one you will be chaperoning and his or her therapist.

Forgiveness Statement

I, _____, do hereby forgive you, _____, for the hurt I feel about your sexual behavior problem. By *forgive*, I mean that I will remember everything I know about your sexual behavior problem but I will not let that knowledge control my feelings. I will talk with you reasonably about your sexual behavior problem and chaperon you to the best of my ability. I have forged this forgiveness so that we can share a healthy relationship. I care about you and will help you.

Here is a brief summary of my understanding of your sexual behavior problem:

_____

_____

I accept you and I accept that you have a sexual behavior problem. Here's what I mean when I say this:

_____

_____

The fact that I can forgive you does not minimize your sexual behavior problem. You have a serious problem that can affect many lives. The way it has changed me and others is:

_____

_____

In return for my forgiveness, I ask that you commit to treatment and work hard to ensure that you have **NO NEW VICTIMS**.

_____   _____

Signature   Date

Myths about Sexual Behavior Problems

Individuals with sexual behavior problems come from all walks of life. The individual with sexual behavior problems can be of any race, religion, or color. Individuals with sexual behavior problems can be young, old, or anywhere in between.

Men are more likely than women to have sexual behavior problems but women aren't excluded. People who dropped out of school may have sexual behavior problems, so may scholars. Income doesn't matter. Ethnicity doesn't matter. As with so many other things, each person with a sexual behavior problem is unique. Contrary to what you see on TV, you cannot tell if a person has a sexual behavior problem just by looking at them.

Most people think they know a great deal about sexual behavior problems but what they know are the myths that have been passed around on the Internet and in the media. The following is a list of the common myths about individuals with sexual behavior problems.

HINT: All of these myths are false...

Myth 1: The individual with sexual behavior problems is a dirty old man.

Truth: The majority of individuals with sexual behavior problems are under the age of thirty-five when their problem comes to light. After their problem is revealed, most individuals with sexual behavior problems will report that they started using inappropriate sexual behavior in their teens. Very few individuals suddenly begin using inappropriate sexual behavior when they are old but it does happen.

Myth 2: The individual with sexual behavior problems victimizes strangers.

Truth: This is probably the most disappointing truth. In reality, the individual with sexual behavior problems usually knows the victim. For example, scientists studying illegal sexual behavior have found that, in about 9 out of 10 cases, the victim and the individual with the sexual behavior problem knew each other. Very few individuals with sexual behavior problems knew their victim for less than 24 hours before having sexual contact with them.

Myth 3: The individual with sexual behavior problems is retarded or mentally ill.

Truth: When people do something bad, it is natural to think there must be something mentally wrong with them. This is often not true. Individuals with sexual behavior problems can have low or high intelligence. A person's intelligence level cannot create or prevent sexual behavior problems. As for mental illness, scientists have found that very few individuals with sexual behavior problems have a mental illness. These same scientists have also found that there is no mental illness that is responsible for most or all of the different types of sexual behavior problems.

Myth 4: The individual with sexual behavior problems used inappropriate sexual behavior because he or she was drunk or high.

Truth: Research shows that very few individuals with sexual behavior problems were using drugs or alcohol at the time of their act of inappropriate sexual behavior. You cannot get the desire to commit any inappropriate sexual act from a can of beer, bottle of wine, or puff of marijuana. When a person is intoxicated or high, inhibitions drop and urges and desires come out more easily, but alcohol and drugs do not create the urge or cause the behavior. The urge for sexual misconduct was in the person before using alcohol or drugs.

Myth 5: Individuals with sexual behavior problems are sexually frustrated.

Truth: While lack of appropriate sex may increase the desire to have sex, the individuals still have a choice about the type of sex they have. Many individuals with sexual behavior problems have a willing sexual partner and an active sexual life. Yet, they still engage in inappropriate sexual behaviors. For example, scientists have found that some men who commit incest have sex with their wife in the same timeframe as molesting their children. The same is true for rapists and individuals who use pornography to excess.

Myth 6: As time passes, the individual with sexual behavior problems will engage in increasingly harmful or dangerous sexual behavior.

14

Truth: Scientists have found little evidence that an individual with sexual behavior problems becomes more extreme over time. Most individuals with sexual behavior problems may exhibit more than one type of sexual misconduct. But, generally, those with problems pursue activities that remain either violent or non-violent, depending on their original tendency. For example, an individual with sexual behavior problems who starts out exposing might become a Peeping Tom. This individual starts out committing a nonviolent sexual act and continues to be nonviolent. On the other hand, violent individuals with sexual behavior problems often start out violent and tend to stay violent.

Myth 7: You can find most individuals with sexual behavior problems lurking in the shadows at parks or malls.

Truth: Unfortunately, you can find most individuals with sexual behavior problems anywhere…at your holiday meal, family gathering, church social, or neighborhood block party. Most individuals with sexual behavior problems are normal people living normal lives, except for their sexual behavior problem.

Myth 8: Women do not have sexual behavior problems.

Truth: Most individuals with sexual behavior problems are, indeed, male but women can have sexual behavior problems, too. The biggest concern about females with sexual behavior problems is that we tend to minimize the behavior or dismiss it. Female sexual behavior problems can be just as harmful to them and their victims as men's sexual behavior problems. All sexual behavior problems are destructive, regardless of whether the individual is male or female.

Myth 9: Once a sex offender always a sex offender

Truth: Research has shown that once a sex offender is caught and exposed publicly, these individuals are very unlikely to have a new sexual offense. Comparing sex offenders to nonsexual offenders reveals that nonsexual offenders (such a burglars or drug offenders) are 10 to 12 more likely than sex offenders to have a new offense. Then there is the matter of treatment. There *is* effective treatment for individuals with sexual behavior problems. But it requires a thought change on the part of the individual with the problem. It also requires them to be honest with themselves and learn effective coping skills. One research study after another has proven that the right type of treatment can reduce the risk of sexual behavior problems by as much as 40 to 50 percent. Even though treatment can be effective, it is not easy. There are no magic pills and there are no guarantees that it will work in every situation. But, with work, it is possible.

Myth 10: A person has to wait to commit a sexual offense to get into treatment for sexual behavior problems.

Truth: Treatment for sexual behavior problems is, in great part, about prevention, i.e., *No New Victims!* Some treatment is aimed at rehabilitation prevention, which means the individual has already created a victim by using inappropriate sexual behavior. However, there are many, many individuals involved in treatment aimed at primary prevention. For example, some individuals who have never used inappropriate sexual behavior with another person enter treatment with the goal of making sure they never do.

The most important thing you can learn from these myths is that you cannot look at a person and know whether that person has sexual behavior problems. Most individuals with sexual behavior problems blend right into our society, community, and even our family.

Assessment: Myth Busters

1. Before learning about the myths, which myths did you think were true?

2. Specifically, which myths, if any, did you think were true about the person you will be chaperoning?

3. Now that you know about the myths, how does that change the way that you look at the individual you will be chaperoning?

Why Does a Person Engage in Inappropriate Sexual Behavior?

We are a long way from knowing exactly why people have sexual behavior problems. But here are a few things we do know…

❖ Everybody is different. Each individual with sexual behavior problems has a uniquely personal reason for using inappropriate sexual behavior.

❖ The way a person thinks can lead them to use inappropriate sexual behavior. For example, many individuals with sexual behavior problems minimize the harm caused by the behavior, so that they can justify it. They know that the behavior is inappropriate, but reason that "it's not *that* bad."

❖ Using inappropriate sexual behavior is not an accident, it is a choice. Each individual with a sexual behavior problem chooses to use a specific inappropriate sexual behavior at a specific time. Some activities are the response to an immediate impulse, others are carefully planned. But all are intentional.

Even though each person is unique, there are some common motives. The research that is discussed below may provide important insight into the individual you will be chaperoning. Keep your mind open as you learn about these motives. The more you learn, the better chaperon you will be.

Motives for Sexual Contact with Children and Teens

There are four common motives used by adults who have sexual contact with children and teenagers. Sometimes an adult might be driven by more than one of these motives.

Emotional Partner: Adults with this motive feel emotionally on the same level as the child or teen and believe that they are in an equal relationship with the youth. They feel that they can relate to the child or teen as a peer and may tell you that they have the same interests as the child. Those who use this motive imagine that the child is their equal partner. This individual justifies sexual contact with the minor by saying things like, "*I know Amy is only eleven but she is so mature. She is as mature as any adult I deal with. Sex is a normal part of an equal relationship. Amy can make up her mind. She is just as mature as me.*"

Adults who view children as emotional partners use a mental technique called "*Growing the Child Up & Growing Myself Down.*" This mental technique allows these adults to look at the children as grown-up and look at themselves as much younger, so they can meet on an equal level. In this fiction, they become equal partners and sex is just one part of the "equal relationship."

Sexual Arousal: Sexual arousal refers to sexual excitement. Some adults are only, or primarily, sexually aroused by children. In clinical terms, these individuals are called Exclusive Pedophiles (EP). These individuals are not sexually aroused by adults, or if they do experience sexual arousal with adults, it is a very mild sexual arousal. It is important to understand what this means. The EP, who is only or primarily sexually aroused by children, will probably never have a satisfying sexual relationship with an adult. Very few individuals who have sexual contact with children or teens are EP; perhaps only 3%.

Blockage: Most people who use blockage as a motive have normal sexual desires for adult sexual partners. These people like to have sex with other adults but feel that the opportunity for normal sex is blocked. So, when the person finds the path to normal sex blocked, the individual tries another path. In other words, if the person can't have sex in the desired way, that person will choose to use inappropriate sex, e.g., sexual contact with a child, excessive use of pornography, or use of prostitutes, spending a great deal of money at topless bars, to name a few.

It is common for those with incest behavior problems to be driven by the Blockage Motive. For example, a husband and wife may be having relationship difficulties. The husband still wants sex with an adult female but he feels that it is too difficult to have sex with his wife. He thinks his path to sexual contact with his wife is blocked. So, he takes the easy way out. Instead of working through the issues with his wife, he may choose to have sexual contact with his child or stepchild. In another example, individuals whose sexual behavior problem is excessive use of legal pornography often may also have "blockage" as their motive.

Loss of Self-Control: If an individual's motive for inappropriate sexual behavior is a lack of self-control, sexual misconduct probably occurs when the person is emotionally vulnerable, such as being exhausted, angry, or in another uncomfortable mood state. The loss of self-control does not create a desire for sexual misconduct. It simply allows the desire for sexual misconduct to be transformed into behavior. The desire for sexual misconduct must already be in the person for it to come out during times of low self-control. So, rather than a true motivator, it is, more accurately, a facilitator.

The researchers who defined these motives were studying adults who had sexual contact with children or teens. However, these motives can apply to individuals with a variety of sexual behavior problems, such as excessive use of pornography, topless bars, massage parlors, or impersonal sex.

Common Motives of Rapists

When you think of a rapist, don't think of the dramatic serial rapist you see on TV. The motives below also apply to individuals who use date rape, spousal rape, or sexual harassment. Research has identified two common motives for those who force or coerce another adult into sexual activity.

Power: Those who use a power motive as the basis for forced sexual contact are doing this to prove to themselves that they are powerful. This person has low self-esteem and feels insecure. By sexually dominating another person, those with sexual behavior problems can look back on the sexual episode to prove that they are powerful. In addition, since sex is gratifying, the pleasure from the sexual excitement can temporarily reduce feelings of self-doubt or inadequacy.

Anger: Anger is a complicated emotion. There are two general ways that it can be a motive for forced sexual contact:

a) **Anger Displacement**: This motive involves redirecting the anger felt for one person toward another. For example, a man may be angry with his wife. So, he goes to a bar, picks up a woman, and drives to an isolated spot where he forces her to have sex. When forcing the woman he met at the bar to have sex, he is motivated by his anger at his wife. *"All women are alike. That @#%& deserves it!"* Once he has finished having sex with his victim, he feels less angry and more in control.

b) **Sadism**: Anger is part of the complex motive of a sadist. A sadist is someone who gets pleasure, sometimes sexual pleasure, from the suffering or humiliation of another person. The more the other person suffers, the more sexually aroused the sadist becomes.

As you can see, there are many different, sometimes contradictory, motives for inappropriate sexual behavior. Learning what motivates the individual you will be chaperoning will greatly improve your effectiveness as a chaperon. Knowing this will help you better understand the urges the person is trying to control or eliminate and what may trigger the unwanted behavior(s). Anything you can do to help them control or eliminate their motives for sexual misconduct will help them eliminate their problematic behavior. As a result, there will be **No New Victims**.

Assessment: Can You Find the Motive?

1. Which of the motives do you think apply to the person you will be chaperoning?

2. Do you understand how the research on motives can apply to anyone with a sexual behavior problem?

3. Have you and the person you will be chaperoning talked about his or her motives? If so, what was said?

4. To the individual, you will be chaperoning, these behaviors "make sense" because he or she has developed rationalizations around their motives. As a chaperon, do you think that you will be able to assume a non-judgmental approach while, at the same time, providing wise companionship? What will you say to yourself to help you with this?

Patterns of Sexual Misconduct

Scientists have been studying sexual misconduct for a long time. Some of their discoveries may be useful for you as a chaperon.

The Age Sexual Misconduct Begins: Most individuals with sexual behavior problems begin using sexually inappropriate behavior while in adolescence. By age 18:

- ❖ Seventy percent of those who have sexual contact with male preteens or teens have committed their first inappropriate sexual act.

- ❖ Fifty percent of all who use forced or coerced sexual contact will have engaged in their first act of forced or coerced sex.

Although most individuals start acting out sexually when they are young, there is also the other side of the coin. Thirty percent of men who have sexual contact with male preteens and teens and fifty percent of men who use force do not commit their first inappropriate act until after they are 18. In fact, some do not commit their first act of inappropriate sexual behavior until they are elderly.

Most Begin with a Certain Behavior and Stick with it: Most individuals with sexual behavior problems start with inappropriate sexual behavior that they find gratifying and then repeat that behavior. For example, 85 percent of men who prefer sexual contact with teens or children start with that behavior. About 44 percent of men who prefer forced or coerced sexual behavior use that type of behavior the first time they sexually act out. In the vast majority of cases, individuals with sexual behavior problems do <u>not</u> start with mild sexual misconduct and then evolve into violent sexual behavior.

In one of the most interesting research studies of sexual behavior problems, researchers asked volunteers from the community to participate in a survey. While some of the participants were on probation or parole, most of those who participated in the study had never had a legal problem due to their sexual behavior. The following is a summary of these research findings. The study was composed solely of men. Most of them had never been in trouble with the law when they participated in the survey.

Crossover: Most who responded to the survey said that while they had a favorite type of sexual behavior, they would also "crossover" and to a different type of sexual behavior.

Crossover by Men Who Have Sexual Contact with Children/Teens	Percentage
Sexual contact with a teen or child	100
Exhibitionism	30
Rape	17
Voyeurism	14
Frottage (sexual touching without consent)	9
Sadism	6
Cross Dressing	1
Obscene Phone Calls or Public Masturbation	0

Crossover by Men Who Use Coercive or Forced Sexual Contact with Other Adults	Percentage
Forced or coerced sexual contact with other adults	100
Sexual contact with teens or children	51
Exhibitionism	29
Voyeurism	20
Frottage (sexual touching without consent)	12
Sadism	11
Cross Dressing	6
Obscene Phone Calls	5

Research on crossover behaviors provides chaperons with important information. It shows that a chaperon cannot just watch the individual being chaperoned for the type of sexual problem that landed them in treatment. Rather, a chaperon must watch for any and all types of sexual misconduct. It is the job of the person you are chaperoning to tell you about their preferred types of sexual misconduct and, together, you can guard against those behaviors so the individual can reach the goal of **No New Victims**.

Sexual Arousal: Based on the survey of individuals in the community, researchers learned that most individuals with sexual behavior problems have normal sexual arousal. Even those individuals with the most severe types of sexual behavior problems, like rapists and child molesters, have elements of normal sexual arousal. For example, one scientist found that 99 percent of the rapists studied and 87 percent of the child molesters were attracted to adults of the opposite sex. This means that these men started with normal sexual arousal and learned to be attracted to harmful or abusive sexual behavior. That is good news because if a person can learn a behavior, they can also unlearn the behavior; they can change.

Rate of Acting Out: The survey of individuals in the community, many of whom were not involved in the legal system, shows that the type of sexual misconduct a person prefers determines how often that individual engages in sexual misconduct.

For example, individuals who prefer to expose or peep, repeatedly engage in these acts. Possibly, because it may be seen as a harmless behavior and requires little effort or planning. On the other hand, individuals whose preferred form of sexual misconduct requires physical contact with another person engage in fewer sexually inappropriate acts. The different rates of acting out are in the table below.

Type of Sexual Misconduct	Median Number of Lifetime Victims
Male child victim outside the family	4
Female child victim outside the family	1
Male child victim in the family	1

Female child victim in the family	1
Rape	1
Voyeurism	30
Frottage (sexual touching without consent)	30
Exhibitionism	35
Public Masturbation	90

You should learn two things from the table above. First, if a sexual abuse perpetrator has to lay hands on a victim (e.g., child molesting), then that perpetrator will have few victims. On the other hand, if a sexual abuse perpetrator has a hands-off deviant sexual behavior, it means the perpetrator will not have to touch the victim (e.g., exposing). Hands-off offenders have a lot more victims than hands-on offenders.

The second thing you should notice about the information in the table above is that half of the people who commit hands-on offenses (rape and child molesting) only have one victim. This is true for all hands-on offenders except those who victimize male children who are not incest victims. This is good news because it means about half the people who get chaperoned will only have one victim. This will make it easier for that person to reach the goal of **No More Victims**. It will make your job easier as a chaperon, too.

When you think about how the scientific research applies to the individual you will be chaperoning, you might feel a bit apprehensive or discouraged. That is not the intent. This information is provided to help you act with more care, wisdom, and understanding. In other words, the information is intended to make you a better chaperon, so you can help the one you are chaperoning have **No New Victims**.

Assessment: Do You Know the Patterns?

1. All of the research cited in this lesson was based on a community survey and most of the men who participated in the survey never had legal problems. Does this mean that this research does not apply to men with legal problems? Explain your answer.

2. How old are most individuals with sexual behavior problems when they start using inappropriate sexual behavior?

3. What is crossover?

4. Why does a chaperon need to know about crossover?

5. Take a look at the table, which type of child molester has the most victims?

6. What percentage of rapists also molest children?

7. What percentage of child molesters also commit rape?

8. How is the information about rates and frequency of cases useful to the chaperon?

Stepping into Trouble

Inappropriate sexual behavior does not just happen. An individual takes specific steps before engaging in sexual misconduct. Each of the stages below is one in which the individual thinks, feels, or acts. This cascade of thoughts, feelings, and actions is referred to as the "Stair Steps".

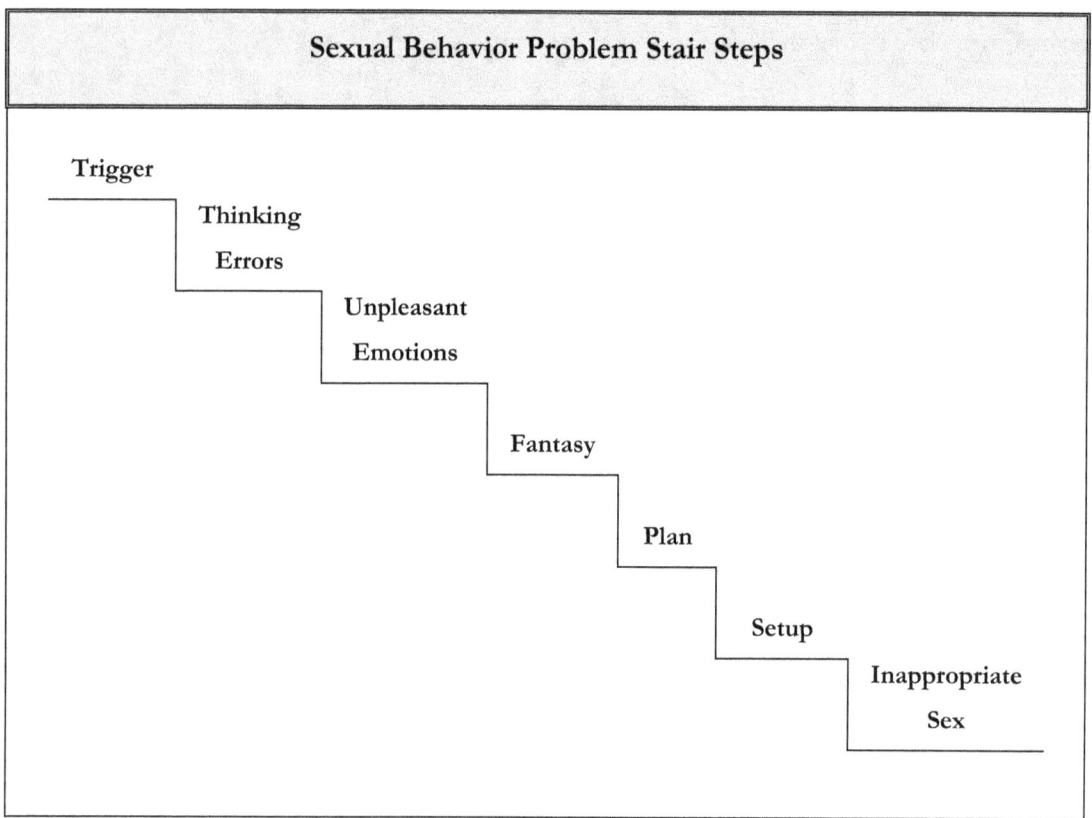

For some, traveling these steps may take days, weeks, months, or even years. While others, especially those with impulse control issues, may fall down the stairs in an instant. It is rare, but some individuals stop at one of the steps and never descend to action.

As a chaperon, it is important to know that sexual misconduct doesn't just happen. The individual you will be chaperoning knows this. You need to learn it, too.

It is important to understand that the individual you will be chaperoning made choices and took certain actions, which led to the sexual problem. Sexual behavior problems are not accidents or mistakes. A sexual behavior problem is a choice, for which they, and they alone, are responsible.

If you know what to look for, you will be better able to help the individual you will be chaperoning. You can use knowledge of the Stair Steps to know whether or not the individual you are chaperoning is actually on one of the steps.

Triggers

An individual does not get on the Stair Steps until a trigger happens. Many think that a trigger is something sexual but it is not. A trigger is a stressor such as conflict, disappointment, or exhaustion. Just about anything stressful can be a trigger.

If stress is well managed or reduced, there is a decreased chance that it will trigger the Stair Step responses. That is why it is important for you and the individual you will be chaperoning to talk about the stress and challenges in his or her life. Ideally, the individual being chaperoned will bring up the problems but, at times, you may need to start the conversation. Here are some things to watch and discuss.

- ❖ Conflict at work or in important relationships

- ❖ Money problems

- ❖ Illness

- ❖ Not taking care of himself or herself

- ❖ Family members under stress

- ❖ Death of a loved one

- ❖ Job loss

- ❖ Moving

- ❖ Problems with being on the public registry (if the person has to register)

❖ Dealing with restrictions of supervision (if the person is in the legal system)

❖ Difficulties in treatment

❖ New medications or adjustments in current medications

Thinking Errors

Thoughts are not facts, even though we often treat them like they are. Thoughts are mental representations of the world that can be accurate or inaccurate. Wildly inaccurate thoughts are called "Thinking Errors." Those working with individuals with sexual behavior problems have identified more than sixty different types of thinking errors. A few of the more common thinking errors are listed below:

❖ **My Way**: I know the "right" way to do things but I want to do things my way, even if it means breaking social norms, rules, or laws.

❖ **Selfish**: I don't care if I hurt others while meeting my needs.

❖ **Entitlement**: The world owes me. If I don't get what I think I should get, I will just take it.

❖ **Minimize**: The bad things I do are not so bad.

❖ **Helpless**: I'm really not in control of my life. I am just a victim of fate, chance, or other people.

❖ **Poor Me**: Feel sorry for me. I've had a rough time (or life).

Unpleasant Emotions

Thinking errors, in turn, cause the individual to have unpleasant feelings. There are four basic emotions: happiness, anger, sadness, and fear. Thinking errors usually result in one of the unpleasant emotions.

Fantasy

When anyone experiences unpleasant emotions, they naturally want to feel better. For this reason, the individual starts to imagine and fantasize about things that might make them feel better. Some of the fantasies will be sexual fantasies.

Plan

This is a turning point because the individual has made a decision to act. Once the individual decides to give in to the sexual fantasies, they start to plan how to accomplish the sexual act.

Setup or Grooming

Next, the individual will set up the situation so they can achieve the inappropriate sexual behavior.

Setup occurs when the individual tries to isolate and exploit a potential victim. For example, if the individual's sexual behavior problem is excessive use of Internet porn, the setup may be to find alone time and avoid those who might stop them.

In some cases, setup is referred to as "grooming." It is difficult to detect grooming because grooming behaviors are typically behaviors that may be performed by anyone, such as being nice to someone, hugging, giving gifts, and so on.

A word of caution…when it comes to grooming behavior, focus your attention only on the individual you will be chaperoning. If someone does not have a sexual behavior problem and you accuse them of grooming, you may be wrong and it could cause serious harm, sometimes even legal issues.

In general, there are certain categories of behavior that someone may use to groom. Keep in mind that a particular individual may never use all of these behaviors or may use different behaviors at different times.

1. **Limit Testing:** Increase intimacy with the potential victim to see if they are receptive or can be manipulated. An individual may test several potential victims to determine which is the most vulnerable.

    <u>Signs of Testing</u>: Increased intimacy, such as touching, sexual talk and so on.

2. **Building Trust**: Build trust with the potential victim. The crafty individual may also build a trusting relationship with the prospective victim's family or friends.

   <u>Signs of Trust Building</u>: Give presents; let the potential victim borrow, play with, or use the individual's personal belongings; tell the potential victim they are special; assure the potential victim that the relationship is positive and normal.

3. **Isolation**: Isolate the victim. The individual will arrange situations to be alone with the potential victim. He or she tries to make it seem as if being alone with the victim is natural.

   <u>Signs of Isolation</u>: Individual goes places alone with the potential victim; arranges situations to be alone in a home, car or other secluded place with the potential victim; tucks the potential victim in at night; sleeps with the potential victim; monopolizes the potential victim's time; gets upset when the potential victim isn't around.

4. **Secrecy**: Tell the potential victim that their relationship can continue only if their activities remain secret.

   <u>Signs of Secrecy</u>: The individual asks the potential victim to keep secrets; the individual praises the victim for keeping secrets; and sometimes, but rarely, the individual threatens the potential victim to ensure they keep secrets. (Most victims do not keep secrets when threatened.)

5. **Boundary Violation**: Increasing physical contact with the potential victim. The escalating physical contact always violates the potential victim's privacy and personal space.

   <u>Sign of Boundary Violations</u>: Backrubs, tickling, wrestling, horseplay, discussing sex, or showing sexual images to the potential victim.

Inappropriate Sex

If the stages of the Stair Steps are not interrupted, the individual engages in inappropriate sexual behavior.

It is important that you understand the Stair Steps. This knowledge will help you understand what to watch for when chaperoning. But remember, you are not a cop or enforcer. You are a companion.

Use this information to help the person you are chaperoning make it through tough times and tough situations.

Assessment: Your Individual's Stair Steps

1. What stressors (triggers) do you think the person you will be chaperoning has in his or her life right now?

2. What are some signs of grooming that the individual you are chaperoning might show?

3. Who are the high-risk persons that the person you are chaperoning might groom?

Being an Effective Member of the Treatment Team

Therapy for sexual misconduct is one of the things that the treatment provider does to teach individuals how to have **No New Victims**. If the individual you will be chaperoning can complete this therapy and reach this goal, a lot of good things will happen, including:

- ❖ No more problems resulting from sexual misbehavior

- ❖ A better relationship with you and with others

- ❖ Improved self-esteem and confidence

- ❖ More successful (If someone is successful in treatment, it affects them to their very core.)

- ❖ No one else will be hurt by their sexual misconduct

Sexual relations are the most intimate interactions two people can share. When individuals learn to engage in sexual relations in a healthy way, they have learned to deal with intimacy in a healthy way. Effective therapy for sexual behavior problems profoundly changes the person. The steps that an individual must take to make a lasting change are not easy but are achievable.

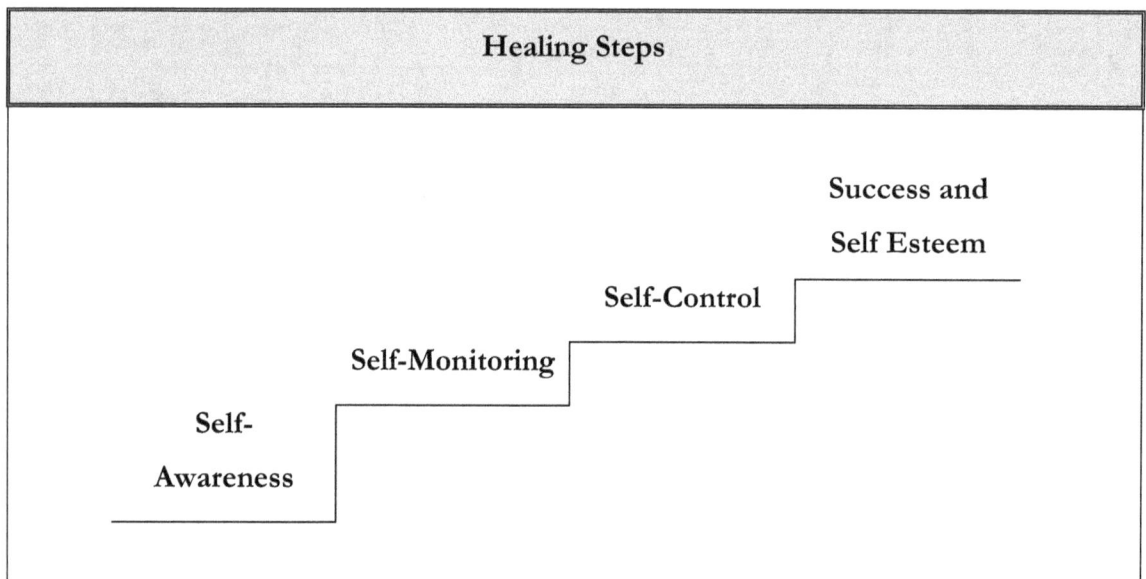

Self-Awareness: To be self-aware is to know yourself. Really, know yourself. Not just your eye color and birth date but your desires, motivations, and triggers. The person with sexual behavior problems must become aware of the thoughts and feelings that created their sexual behavior problem. For true self-awareness, the individual must first admit the desire to use inappropriate sexual behavior. When the person with sexual behavior problems has become honest enough to admit that he or she actually wants to use inappropriate sexual behavior, then true healing can begin.

Self-Monitoring: When you self-monitor, you are watching yourself. Individuals in therapy for sexual behavior problems are asked to monitor their thoughts, feelings, and actions for signs that they might be at risk for engaging in inappropriate sexual behavior. These warning signs for sexual misconduct are often called high-risk situations. As a chaperon, you need to know the high-risk situations for the person you will be chaperoning.

Self-Control: Self-control is the ability to control your behavior, especially your emotions and impulses. This is not easy for anyone, but those with sexual behavior problems are especially challenged by this. Through the course of their therapy, those with sexual behavior problems are taught very specific, proven self-control techniques. You will learn some of these techniques later in this workbook so you can encourage the individual you will be chaperoning to use them when they are needed.

Self-Esteem and Success: When an individual has a level of mastery over the first three steps, he or she will feel a sense of accomplishment and increased confidence. Likewise, when an individual's confidence and self-esteem increase, there is a better chance that the person will succeed in their healing, as well as other parts of his or her life.

This level of success does not come overnight. It requires both willingness and effort to overcome the huge obstacle of a sexual behavior problem. Each step requires hard work and practice. It is rare for someone to complete sexual behavior problem therapy in less than a year. Actually, most people take at least three years to complete this type of treatment. But when someone is successful in treatment for a sexual behavior problem, the changes are deep and lasting.

If the individual you are going to chaperon is successful in treatment for a sexual behavior problem, he or she will have **No New Victims**. And, the odds are that the individual will also be, on the whole, happier and more successful.

Assessment: What Is Therapy Anyway?

1. What is the goal of therapy for sexual behavior problems?

2. What does a person in sexual behavior problem therapy have to do to show self-awareness?

3. What does a person in sexual behavior problem therapy have to do to show self-monitoring?

4. Why does an individual in therapy for sexual behavior problems have to examine his or her inappropriate sexual behavior?

5. Why do you have to know about the inappropriate sexual behavior used by the individual you will be chaperoning?

6. How long do you think the individual you will be chaperoning will be in therapy?

Treatment Team Participation

A treatment team is composed of all of the professionals who provide treatment services to the person with sexual behavior problems. Sometimes, the team may be small, such as when there's only one counselor providing treatment. Other times, such as when the person is in a residential treatment program, the treatment team may be quite large. A residential team may include a counselor, nurse, psychiatrist, trainer, and supervision staff.

To reach the goal of **No More Victims,** a client must first examine his or her inappropriate behavior. The client must examine their motives and desires underlying the sexual misconduct. This will give the client the skills to identify high-risk situations. Once a client has the skill and inclination to be in control in a high-risk situation, they have a greater chance for success.

One of the most difficult things to do in treatment for a sexual behavior problem is to openly examine the inappropriate sexual behavior. Most clients are embarrassed and ashamed. However, this understanding is crucial since the person's past behavior reveals what they need to control.

Clients are not the only ones who get embarrassed by talking about sexual behavior problems. It is not uncommon for Chaperons to get embarrassed too. You may feel embarrassed at times but there is no way to avoid the issue. You may need courage too.

If you want to help a client succeed in this type of therapy, you, too, will need to examine and understand their sexual misconduct. This window into their world can teach you how to better recognize and talk with them about triggers and high-risk situations.

Clients in treatment for sexual behavior problems will have a great deal of written homework to complete. In fact, most clients have to complete an entire therapy workbook before being discharged from treatment. As a chaperon, your involvement in these homework assignments is important. Knowing their training and goals will help you help them every step of the way.

- If the individual has a therapy workbook, read the entire workbook.

- Read all of the assignments completed by the one you will be chaperoning.

- It's perfectly OK for you to help your client complete assignments. No, it's not cheating. Clients must present and discuss all assignments in therapy sessions. If a client shows that he or she does not understand the assignment, it will be obvious. The treatment provider will ask the client to redo the assignment until he or she gets it.

When you become a chaperon, you will join the treatment team. There are four things you will need to do to be a treatment team member:

1. Stick to Your Values

2. Ask Questions

3. Attend Meetings

4. Help with Therapy Assignments

Stick to Your Values

Like most people in treatment for a sexual behavior problem, the one you will be chaperoning was most probably cajoled, encouraged, or required to get treatment. Entering into treatment was probably a compromise, at best, or, at worst, mandated by a family member, criminal court, family court, or Child Protective Services court.

No one likes to be told what to do. It is natural to resist or even be defiant when forced to do something. People forced into treatment for a sexual behavior problem are no exception.

If the one you are chaperoning is resisting treatment, it raises a challenging question for you: **Whose side are you on?**

This is a trick question. It is not a question of _whose_ side you are on. It is a question of _which_ side you are on. Are you on the side of health or sexual behavior problems?

If you are on the side of health, you want the one you chaperon to be a success. This means that there may be times when you will need to remember that, while some of the therapy may be incredibly difficult for the individual you will be chaperoning, letting them slide will hurt rather than help.

To figure out which side you are on, ask yourself one question: **Do I want the individual I will be chaperoning to be happy and successful?** If you answered yes, then you are on the right side.

If the individual you will be chaperoning is resisting therapy, it is only a matter of time before he or she fails. If you help the one you are chaperoning resist therapy, the individual will only fail more quickly.

You can help stop the resistance by being there for the one you will be chaperoning and working with him or her on assignments. (More on that later.) Share the therapy experience and help the person know that he or she is not alone. This will give the one you will be chaperoning a much greater shot at success.

If the individual reaches their therapy goal, he or she will have **No New Victims**. You will have helped this individual become happy and successful. As a bonus, you may have grown too.

Ask Questions

You are probably not an expert in the treatment of sexual behavior problems. Actually, very few mental health professionals are trained experts in this field. If you are like most chaperons-in-training, you are unsure about what you can, or should, do. You might even have some confusion about the treatment program that is sponsoring this chaperon training.

There is only one thing to do when you are confused. Ask questions. Ask members of the treatment team. Ask the individual you will be chaperoning. Ask both. But ask. Proceed with caution when researching your questions on the Internet. There are very few qualified sources on this subject and a very long list of charlatans.

When you have questions, jot them down until you can connect with the individual you will be chaperoning, their treatment provider, or both. Leave room below the questions. When you get an answer, you can include it just below the question. For questions you feel are especially important, you may want to get answers from more than one person. Whenever it makes sense, it can be useful to get answers from both the individual you will be chaperoning and their treatment provider(s).

You need to know that you are not being a pest when you ask questions. You are doing your "job". The more you know, the better you can help.

Attend Meetings

There are two types of meetings that a chaperon may attend: therapy sessions and staffings.

Therapy Sessions. The therapy sessions that you will attend are called individual therapy sessions. As a chaperon, or someone who knows and cares about the individual you will be chaperoning, you can say anything you think might be helpful during these sessions.

It is important to understand that when you attend a therapy session, it is not *your* therapy session. That can be both good and bad news. The good news is that you will not be put on the spot. You won't be required to discuss your personal issues. The bad news is you might need or want therapy. Unfortunately, you will have to go somewhere else for your own therapy.

Staffings. The other type of meeting you will attend is a staffing. A staffing is a meeting of the treatment team—the staff. As a chaperon, your input is crucial. This is your chance to share information with the other members of the treatment team regarding how you think the individual is doing when he or she is not in treatment. What you relate can be used to adjust the course of treatment and improve the person's chance of success.

Help with Therapy Assignments

Treatment is a long journey that is not easily traveled alone. As a chaperon, you can be a supportive companion on this long, and often winding road. You may not ever know how much your participation means to the one you are chaperoning. But being there for them means far more than he or she will probably be able to express.

One important way to participate in the experience is to help with therapy assignments. Helping with the assignments will give you a window into what the individual you are chaperoning is thinking, feeling, and learning. It will also give the person a sounding board for feelings and perceptions. It will offer the opportunity to see the problem from someone else's perspective. Most importantly, the shared experience will help the person feel that, while it is a singular and personal journey, he or she is not alone.

You will likely have a continuing relationship with the person you are chaperoning well past treatment. By 'walking the walk' with the person, you will be able to continue providing appropriate support and encouragement long after the treatment provider(s) are out of the picture. Your ability to help the person in the future will depend on how much you learn while the individual is in treatment. The more you learn, the better you will be able to help.

When you help with assignments…

Learn the important terms, concepts, and ideas in the assignments. Knowing the language will help you communicate more clearly with the individual you will be chaperoning.

Discuss the assignments. Establishing and maintaining an open channel of communication will give you both practice talking frankly and honestly about sexual matters and other important topics. This practice will help the two of you talk about these issues in the future, even after the individual has completed treatment.

Don't worry about whether you are giving too much help with assignments. The important thing is for the individual you will be chaperoning to learn the material. You can't do the work for them. That's their road to travel. But you can provide an abundance of fuel. An individual will only be given credit for an assignment once they can show that they have learned the material.

Chaperon Do's and Don'ts

Helps Individual Succeed	Causes Individuals to Fail
• Help with assignments	• Allow or encourage the individual not to do assignments
• Encourage them to follow rules	• Keep secrets from treatment staff
• Encourage them to be honest	• Allow the individual to break treatment or supervision rules
• Confront when he or she breaks rules	• Deny that the person has a sexual behavior problem
• Meet with treatment staff	
• Talk openly with treatment staff	

Assessment: What Are Your Stumbling Blocks?

1. Does the individual you will be chaperoning do things to force you to pick between him or her and treatment?

2. Do you think that treatment is unfair? Would you like to rescue the one you will be chaperoning from treatment?

3. Does it hurt you to see the one you will be chaperoning struggle with treatment?

4. What are the three things about treatment that you find the most confusing or disagreeable?

5. How do you feel about helping the individual you will be chaperoning with assignments?

Criteria for Being a Chaperon

Just as the individual has to meet certain criteria to be chaperoned, the chaperon has to meet certain criteria to qualify to serve as a chaperon. Some but not all of the criteria that a chaperon could be required to meet include:

1. Has completed chaperon training.

2. Attend therapy sessions.

3. Accept that the individual you chaperon has a sexual behavior problem that resulted in the person undergoing treatment.

4. Do not minimize the seriousness of the individual's sexual behavior problem.

5. Do not make excuses for the person's sexual behavior. Recognize that it was a choice the individual made. Admit that it was something that he or she wanted to do.

6. Admit that the person's sexual behavior caused harm to him- or herself and others.

7. Recognize that the individual could easily resume using problematic sexual behavior; either the same kind that resulted in admission to the treatment program or any other form of sexual behavior problem.

8. If needed, be willing to protect potential victims from the individual you will be chaperoning.

9. Be willing to help the individual deal with high-risk situations.

10. Discuss issues honestly and in a timely manner with the individual's treatment provider and treatment team.

11. Stop serving as a chaperon if, ***for any reason***, you cannot chaperon effectively.

The criteria listed above are just a few examples of those that a potential chaperon must meet. Every person's situation is unique. If you want to know your requirements and the individual's requirements, check with the treatment provider.

If the individual is legally mandated into treatment, also check with the legal authority, such as the probation officer, family court judge, Child Protective Services caseworker, guardian ad litem, or other relevant legal authority.

While it is rare, some individuals must be supervised in high-risk situations for the rest of their lives. Approximately 1% or fewer of all cases involving individuals with sexual behavior problems fall into this category.

There are a variety of reasons for permanent restrictions. Some include: the person has vowed to sexually exploit others; the person is an impulsive, exclusive pedophile; or the person has a mental abnormality that makes it likely that they will sexually harm other people. Some people will need help for the duration of their lives to help ensure they have **NO NEW VICTIMS.**

Remember, the work that you are doing is not only assisting the individual you will be chaperoning but may also be protecting many other people.

Assessment: Are You a Chaperon Yet?

1. Which of the chaperon criteria have you already met?

2. Which of the chaperon criteria do you still need to meet?

3. What is the most difficult thing for you about meeting the criteria to be a chaperon?

Safety and High-Risk Situations

A high-risk situation is any *person, place, or thing* that makes it easy for an individual to resume inappropriate sexual behavior. Be clear, a high-risk situation doesn't cause the individual to use inappropriate sexual behavior. It simply makes sexual misconduct easier or more likely.

The situation cannot be blamed for a person's sexual misconduct. How they choose to act—or not act—is up to the individual.

High-Risk Persons: If someone's inappropriate sexual behavior entailed excessive trips to topless bars, a high-risk person would be anyone who used to accompany the individual to topless bars. If a person engaged in sexual contact with a teenager, teenagers would be high-risk persons.

Someone who doesn't believe that an individual has a sexual behavior problem or could have such a problem in the future may also a high-risk person.

High-Risk Places: If an individual's sexual behavior problem entailed excessive use of online pornography, the Internet would be a high-risk place. If a person's sexual problem was having affairs with people they met in bars, then bars would be a high-risk place. If a person had sexual contact with a child, then high-risk places would be homes where children live, parks, public swimming pools, schools, and any other places where children gather.

High-Risk Things: Anything that increases someone's desire for sexual misconduct can be a high-risk thing. For example, some individuals use pornography to fuel the desire for sexual misconduct. In general, anything that lowers self-control is a high-risk thing, e.g., drugs, alcohol, fatigue, stress, relationship problems, unpleasant emotions, and so on.

If you consider a list of things that can cause someone to lose control, the first that come to mind are probably external triggers, like drugs and alcohol. But emotional triggers can have an enormous impact too. Negative feelings, like anger, sadness, or loneliness, can reduce resistance to performing sexually inappropriate acts.

What does this mean for you as a chaperon? It means that you will want to be in tune with the stress level of the one you are chaperoning. When you notice an increase in stress or personal problems, talk with him or her about these problems. If the individual would like, you may even help strategize solutions.

It is impossible to remove every high-risk situation from someone's life. Eliminating all high-risk situations is not even a goal in treatment. The goal is to help a person learn to *deal effectively* with high-risk situations.

To accomplish this, an individual must do two things. First, the person must learn to recognize his or her high-risk situations. Second, the individual must develop and use safety plans for dealing with these situations.

Helping a person with sexual behavior problems deal with high-risk situations is one of the most important things a chaperon can do. You can help the individual you will be chaperoning deal effectively with high-risk situations by doing the following:

- ❖ Help the individual recognize when he or she is approaching, or in, a high-risk situation.

- ❖ Help the person cope with high-risk situations. The individual will be taught coping skills in treatment. You can help him or her remember the skills and apply them.

- ❖ Encourage and praise the person you are chaperoning when he or she uses coping skills to deal with high-risk situations.

Assessment: Risky Situations

1. What are your individual's high-risk (a) persons; (b) places; and (c) things?

2. How does the one you are chaperoning cope with these high-risk situations?

3. What are the important relationships in the person's life that could become triggers??

Dealing with High-Risk Situations

As part of treatment for sexual behavior problems, individuals are taught how to cope with high-risk situations. Different treatment programs teach different types of coping skills but all coping can be boiled down to one acronym: ACE. **A**void. **C**ope. **E**scape.

Avoid: As a coping skill, avoid means staying away from persons, places, or things that would make it easier to use inappropriate sexual behavior. To use "avoid" as a coping skill, an individual must be <u>smart</u> enough to recognize the high-risk situations and <u>strong</u> enough to stay away.

Escape: On occasion, an individual might be surprised and unexpectedly find themselves in a high-risk situation. For example, a person could be at work and someone shows them a sexual image on a computer. There was no warning. It just happened. In this high-risk situation, the individual must escape, or leave, as quickly as possible.

Cope: You cannot easily avoid or escape when the high-risk situation comes from within, e.g., urges, desires and fantasies. Then, the only option is to cope. All coping skills are mental self-control techniques.

Here are just a few examples of coping skills:

❖ <u>Tunnel Vision/Distraction</u>: Intensely focus on something else.

❖ <u>Golden Rule</u>: Consider, *"Would I want someone else to be thinking of my mother/father/spouse/child in this way?"*

❖ <u>Punishment Scene</u>: Create a reminder list of all of the bad things that happened after sexual misconduct was discovered and then play a mental movie of these things happening again. Or expand the scenario to the worst-case outcome.

There are many more coping techniques. Ask the individual you will be chaperoning about the coping skills he or she has learned and which work best.

As a chaperon, safety is your first concern. Safety for the individual you will be chaperoning, of course. But also, safety for yourself and any potential victims.

In treatment, the individual you will be chaperoning will be required to create and abide by a certain set of safety rules. Because each individual is unique, the individual you will be chaperoning may have different rules from those below. But these will give you a good idea of how safety rules are structured.

Safety with Children

- ❖ Do not be alone with a child.

- ❖ Do not tuck a child into bed without the chaperon present.

- ❖ Do not sleep with a child.

- ❖ Do not have a child sit on your lap.

- ❖ Do not check on a child in the middle of the night.

- ❖ Lock bathroom doors when someone is using the bathroom.

- ❖ Children's rooms should have locks on the door that can be locked from the inside.

- ❖ Put alarms on bedroom doors and activate them at night.

- ❖ Before entering a restroom, the chaperon should make sure there are no children in the restroom.

- ❖ When riding in a car, make sure the individual does not sit next to a child.

Assignment: Creating Safety Rules

Although you won't be creating the individual you will be chaperoning's safety rules, the following exercise will help you understand the process.

- ❖ Write three rules for the person you will be chaperoning. Write one rule each for a high-risk person, place, or thing.

Steps for Increased Contact with Potential Victims

Once the Chaperon Contract has been approved, life does not radically change. You and the person you are chaperoning take gradual steps and slowly begin to deal with high-risk situations. Usually, there are four steps to increased contact with potential victims.

1. Chaperoned contact with potential victims at home.
2. Chaperoned contact with potential victims away from home.
3. Unsupervised contact with own children at home.
4. Unsupervised contact with potential victims away from home.

There are specific criteria that you and the person you are chaperoning must meet to move from one step to the next. It is important to realize that it takes time to move from one step to the next. It is also important to realize that some clients never get to Step 3 or Step 4.

Success at lower steps will determine success at the higher steps. To pass from one step to the next, the person you are chaperoning must prove his or her success by passing a polygraph exam. The polygraph exam is conducted to help determine if the person you are chaperoning has met all the goals and has successfully used self-control techniques to ensure that there are **No More Victims**.

Step One: Chaperoned Contact with Potential Victims at Home

This is the first step in the chaperon process that allows the person you are chaperoning to have contact with potential victims at home. The potential victims are any children living in the home where the person you are chaperoning will have chaperoned visits. Usually, the potential victims are the client's children or stepchildren.

Even though the first step will allow the person you are chaperoning to have contact with potential victims at home, under your supervision, the initial contact with potential victims is always at the treatment provider's office. The client, chaperon, and any children living in the home must meet the following criteria before the client is permitted to have contact with potential victims at home.

Client	• Approved Chaperon Contract • No denial of responsibility for the offense • Has knowledge of triggers for offense • Has self-control skills to deal with triggers and urges • Willing to put the needs of potential victims first • Open to supervision and feedback from the chaperon • If any child in the home is a victim of the client, the client must have completed clarification prior to beginning chaperoned contact with that child.
Chaperon	• Believes that the client committed the instant offense • Believes that the client could reoffend or still use deviant sex • Is willing to protect potential victims • Knows the client's triggers and urges • Has successfully completed Chaperon Training
Potential Victims	• Has completed outcry training • Able and willing to report the client's misconduct to the chaperon • Assertive enough to say no to the client • Willing to disclose if the client engages in grooming or abuse • If any child in the home has been a victim of the client, the child must have completed sex abuse trauma counseling and shown the following: (a) reduction in victim thinking errors; (b) wants the client in the home; (c) has positive feelings about the client without minimizing; (d) does not have flashbacks or regress around the client; and, (e) has completed clarification with the client

Step Two: Chaperoned Contact with Potential Victims Away from Home

This is the second step in the chaperon process. This step is taken after the person you are chaperoning has demonstrated responsible use of the Chaperon Contract at home. The next step is for the person you are chaperoning to be able to go to high-risk areas outside the home, while you chaperon him or her. You and the person you are chaperoning must meet the following criteria before the person you are chaperoning is permitted to have contact with potential victims away from home.

Client	<ul><li>Progress in all areas of treatment</li><li>No longer masturbates to deviant fantasies</li><li>Has at least three well-developed coping skills for dealing with high-risk situations</li><li>Has exhibited compliance with Step One in the Chaperon Process.</li><li>Has demonstrated openness to the Chaperon</li><li>Has demonstrated willingness to follow Chaperon's instructions</li></ul>
Chaperon	<ul><li>Attends all therapy sessions as requested by treatment staff</li><li>Communicates the client's successes and failures with the Chaperon Contract to treatment staff</li><li>Exhibits a willingness to protect potential victims</li><li>Does not make excuses for or minimize the client's noncompliance with the Chaperon Contract</li><li>Has successfully performed the Chaperon Role for two months</li></ul>

Step Three: Unsupervised Contact with Potential Victims at Home

In the third step of the chaperon process, the person you are chaperoning continues to be chaperoned in high-risk areas away from home. However, the person you are chaperoning can now begin unsupervised contact with potential victims at home. Unsupervised contact with potential victims is limited to the person you are chaperoning's family and relatives. Unsupervised contact does not extend to friends of potential victims or potential victims outside of the family.

As with the other steps in the chaperon process, the person you are chaperoning can only take this step if he or she has demonstrated success in the prior steps. Success is determined by meeting specific criteria and passing a polygraph exam. You, the person you are chaperoning, and potential victims must meet the following criteria before the person you are chaperoning is permitted to have unsupervised contact with potential victims at home.

Client	<ul><li>Progress in all areas of treatment</li><li>The client is not a pedophile, i.e., exclusive or primary sexual attraction is towards children.</li><li>Actively helps other group members during group therapy sessions</li><li>Demonstrates a transfer of knowledge and coping skills from the therapy setting to other aspects of life, e.g., home, work, and recreation</li><li>Has exhibited compliance with Step Two in the Chaperon Process</li><li>Has demonstrated openness to the Chaperon and a willingness to follow Chaperon's instructions</li><li>Passed a polygraph exam regarding compliance with the Chaperon Contract</li></ul>
Chaperon	<ul><li>Attends all therapy sessions as requested by treatment staff</li><li>Communicates the client's successes and failures with the Chaperon Contract to treatment staff</li><li>Exhibits a willingness to protect potential victims</li><li>Does not make excuses for or minimize the client's noncompliance with the Chaperon Contract</li><li>Has successfully performed the Chaperon Role for four months</li></ul>
Potential Victims	<ul><li>Has met with the treatment provider and demonstrated a willingness to be alone with the client</li><li>Able and willing to report the client's misconduct to the chaperon or the treatment staff</li></ul>

	<ul><li>Understands that no other children (friends or relatives) can be home when the chaperon is not at home</li><li>Assertive enough to say NO to the client</li><li>Willing to disclose if the client engages in grooming or abuse</li></ul>

Step Four: Unsupervised Contact with Potential Victims away from Home

This is the last step in the chaperon process. In this step, the person you are chaperoning is permitted to have unsupervised contact with potential victims outside of the home. As with the prior steps, permission to be placed on this step and to stay on this step depends on the person you are chaperoning's behavior. It may be the most important thing that the person you are chaperoning can do to prove that he or she should be allowed to stay on this step is for him or her to pass a polygraph exam.

Client	<ul><li>Progress in all areas of treatment</li><li>The client is not a pedophile, i.e., exclusive or primary sexual attraction is towards children.</li><li>Demonstrates a transfer of knowledge and coping skills from the therapy setting to other aspects of life, e.g., home, work, and recreation</li><li>Has exhibited compliance with Step Three in the Chaperon Process</li><li>Has demonstrated openness to the Chaperon</li><li>Passed polygraph exam regarding compliance with the Chaperon Contract</li></ul>
Chaperon	<ul><li>Attends all therapy sessions as requested by treatment staff</li><li>Communicates the client's successes and failures with the Chaperon Contract to treatment staff</li><li>Exhibits a willingness to protect potential victims</li><li>Does not make excuses for or minimize the client's noncompliance with the Chaperon Contract</li><li>Has successfully performed the Chaperon Role for four months</li></ul>

Conclusion

There are four steps that the person you are chaperoning will take. It might take the person you are chaperoning more than twelve months to take all of the steps. The person you are chaperoning must take these steps while he or she is in treatment. If there are problems, you and the person you are chaperoning can discuss these problems with the treatment provider. Additionally, the treatment provider can use the polygraph exam to determine if there are hidden problems. If there are problems, these problems will be discovered while the person you are chaperoning is in treatment. You and the treatment provider can solve these problems before the person you are chaperoning leaves the support of a treatment program.

Reduced Restrictions. Not Reduced Effort.

When restrictions are reduced, it is important to pay special attention to the individual you will be chaperoning's coping skills and relationships. Effective coping skills and healthy relationships are the most important ingredients for ensuring **No New Victims**.

Coping Skills: Monitor how the individual you will be chaperoning copes when he or she is in a high-risk situation. If the person you are chaperoning has challenges, help them. If useful, remind them of the coping skills they have learned. When the individual has successes, help him or her identify what worked so that the skill can be pulled out of the tool belt again later.

Relationships: Interpersonal relations are a challenge for everyone and may be amplified for those with sexual behavior problems. Relationships can be a source of stress or comfort. Maintaining healthy relationships at home, at work, and with friends is the responsibility of the individual you will be chaperoning. Your job is to help…when it is appropriate.

When it comes to relationships, there is a fine line between helping and annoying. You may want to guide the individual you will be chaperoning at every turn, but respecting his or her emotional space will go a long way in maintaining a healthy relationship. Do your best to keep an open flow of communications and realize that, while you may not have a sexual behavior problem, you don't know everything.

On the flip side, don't let your imperfections hold you back from providing valuable input. As a chaperon, it is important that you jump in and get involved in the person's life. In treatment, the individual has been taught the importance of letting other people help. Give them the opportunity to practice that behavior.

As you and the individual you will be chaperoning move away from treatment into the open world, be kind to the individual you will be chaperoning…and to yourself. Keep in mind that the person you will be chaperoning is not perfect and neither are you. You may both make mistakes. But learn from them and keep moving forward. That said, it is imperative that the two of you continue to ensure that there are **No New Victims**.

Assessment: The Open Road

1. List what you can do to prepare for life after treatment?

2. List what you can discuss with the individual's treatment provider to become a better chaperon?

SECTION TWO: MONITORING THE CHAPERON CONTRACT

The Chaperon Contract

The Chaperon Contract is an agreement among three parties—the individual, the chaperon, and the treatment provider. The Chaperon Contract is written by the individual in treatment and it is composed of rules that the person will follow for dealing with high-risk situations. The purpose of the Chaperon Contract is to give the individual practice dealing with high-risk situations, while receiving support and encouragement from a chaperon and treatment provider.

As mentioned earlier in this workbook, the chaperon is not responsible for policing or enforcing the rules of the Chaperon Contract. The individual is responsible for following the rules. The chaperon accompanies the person into high-risk situations. The chaperon provides support to the one in treatment and communicates with the treatment provider.

Treatment for sexual behavior problems, as we know it today, began in the 1970s. By the 1980s, treatment providers began using chaperon contracts. As you might imagine, from 1980 to present, there have been many versions of the Chaperon Contract.

The individual you are chaperoning may or may not have used the Chaperon Contract format presented below when they completed their Chaperon Contract assignment. The sample Chaperon Contract presented below is provided to give you an idea of what goes into a contemporary Chaperon Contract.

Guidelines for Writing a Chaperon Contract

To complete the Chaperon Contract, the individual must use the following outline. The person is expected to carefully read and respond to each item. As a part of chaperon training, you can read each item and try to imagine the best way to respond given the unique situation of the individual you will be chaperoning.

Keep in mind, **the instructions below are written from the perspective of the individual with a sexual behavior problem**. When you respond to an item, try to respond as you anticipate the individual would respond.

Sample Chaperon Contract

Description of Primary Sexual Behavior Problem: The purpose of this item is to inform chaperons about your primary sexual behavior problem. To do this, you must honestly and completely describe your primary sexual behavior problem. Your primary sexual behavior problem is the sexual behavior problem that caused you to seek treatment or required you to participate in treatment. Your primary sexual behavior problem is probably the problematic sexual behavior that you used most often in the past because it was your preferred sexual behavior. Provide a chronology of this sexual behavior problem. When did it start? How often did you use this behavior? What kind of problems did it cause you and others? If it has ended, when did it end? If it ended due to legal involvement (e.g., family court, CPS court, or criminal court), describe the nature of the legal issues.

Description of Secondary Sexual Behavior Problems: It is rare for an individual to have just one type of sexual behavior problem. Research on crossover suggests that if you have one type of sexual behavior problem you probably have a few others. Your family and friends who become chaperons must know about the other types of sexual behavior problems you have.

It is understood that sharing about your sexual behavior problem(s) will be difficult but it is important. You earn two benefits when you share. First, it helps your family and friends get past any denial they may have. Those close to you may not want to believe that you have a sexual behavior problem. Second, by letting your family and friends know about the past, they will know what to watch for in the future.

Make a list of all of the different types of sexual behavior problems you have had. It is best to do a chronology for each behavior problem.

Warning! You have a constitutional right not to provide information that could result in a legal charge against you. If the sexual behavior you describe is illegal behavior that nobody knows about except you (and perhaps the victim), do not give a date, time, or place when this sexual behavior took place. Do not identify the victim. Your treatment provider has a duty to report any previously unknown illegal sexual behavior. Do not provide your treatment provider with enough information to be charged with a crime.

High-Risk Situations Covered by the Chaperon Contract: A high-risk situation can be a person, place or thing. Develop rules for the high-risk situations you will encounter while using this Chaperon Contract.

List the high-risk people, places, and things to be covered by your chaperon contract.

A. **High-Risk People**: Make a list of the people in your life who could be potential victims. For example, if your primary sexual behavior problem entails sexual contact with a teenage family member, list all of the teenagers and children with whom you are likely to come in contact—even those who are not family members. Be honest, complete, and objective. Even if you do not think that you will sexually exploit them. If they fit your victim profile, list them as a high-risk person.

Second, list all of the people, if any, who may have triggered your urges or desire for sexual misconduct. This is not a chance to transfer blame, but an opportunity for you to be aware of potential challenges.

B. **High-Risk Places:** Use both your responses to questions in this Chaperon Contract, and your imagination, as means for identifying high-risk places. Continuing the example of a person whose sexual offense was with a teenage relative, high-risk places for this person might include such locations as a relative's house where teens/children live, schools, high school sporting events, and other similar places.

C. **High-Risk Things**: High-risk things are situations, activities or other factors that make it easier for you to resume using the inappropriate sexual behavior. For many people, using drugs or alcohol would be a high-risk thing. Looking at sexual images is typically a high-risk thing. Books, movies, magazines, and other forms of entertainment may also pose risks. Special events and holidays may be high-risk things. Feeling angry, tired, lonely, or distressed can be high-risk situations. Make a list of at least five high-risk things in your life right now.

Create rules for each high-risk situation you listed above. As an example, for an individual who sexually exploited a teenaged girl, his eleven-year-old stepdaughter, Amber, could be a high-risk person. Here are some examples of rules that this person might use to manage his contact as it relates to Amber.

Amber is my eleven-year-old stepdaughter. She is a high-risk person because she is a child and will soon be a teenager. My rules for Amber are:

A. *Never sit next to her on the couch; always have my chaperon or someone else sit between us.*

B. *Never physically discipline Amber.*

C. *Never be alone with Amber. Always be with my chaperon when I am around Amber.*

D. *Never tickle, wrestle or play any other physical games with Amber.*

E. *Never sleep in the same room as Amber.*

F. *Put a lock on Amber's door so she can lock the door from the inside. She will sleep with her door locked.*

G. *I will put an electronic motion detector on my door. My wife will activate it when we go to bed and turn it off in the morning when we get up.*

Write your rules for high-risk situations on a separate sheet of paper. Your treatment provider will make copies of your rules for high-risk situations. You will keep a copy with you at all times. So, will your chaperon. You should also post these rules at home, like on the refrigerator.

Signatures and Approval: At the end of your Chaperon Contract, leave space for you, your chaperon and your treatment provider to sign. If you are legally mandated to be in treatment and there is someone with legal authority overseeing your treatment (e.g., probation officer), also create a place for that person to sign.

Above the space where you will sign, write the following statement of agreement:

I agree to abide by the safety rules written in this Chaperon Contract.

Above the space where your chaperon will sign, write the following statement of agreement:

I agree to accompany this individual into the areas covered by this Chaperon Contract and around all high-risk persons, places, and things. I agree to attend therapy sessions with the individual. I agree to report to the treatment provider when the individual does not follow safety guidelines or goes into inappropriate areas not covered by the Chaperon Contract.

The Why Sandwich

It is not a question of *if* a relationship will have problems; it is a question of *when*…and what type of problems will take place. The problems that you and the individual you are chaperoning are likely to have include:

1. **Resentment**: As a chaperon, you may start to resent that you have to accompany the individual everywhere. He or she may resent that you are always watching and always there.

2. **Closed Channel**: The individual may want to keep some things to himself or herself about high-risk situations or problems with sexual thoughts and urges.

3. **Power Play**: The person you will be chaperoning may get into a power struggle with you and try to tell you how to be a chaperon. Or you may overreach and try to advise the individual on matters outside your role as chaperon.

A problem does not have to end a chaperon relationship. Relationships survive, and even thrive, because people work through problems. There is a simple problem solving process, called the "Why Sandwich," that you and the individual you chaperon can use to solve problems you encounter.

The Why Sandwich

The Why Sandwich has its name because there are three steps to this problem-solving process: one "why" question sandwiched between two "what" questions:

1. *What is the problem?*

2. *Why is it a problem?*

3. *What can we do to solve this problem?*

If you and the individual you will be chaperoning become skilled at using the Why Sandwich, you can keep the chaperon relationship from eating your lunch.

What is the Problem?

In this step of the problem-solving process, you must describe the problem in detail. Sometimes, just describing the problem can provide insight into how to solve it. Use the following questions to get started:

- ❖ What is the problem?

- ❖ Where did it happen?

- ❖ Who is involved?

- ❖ How many times has it happened?

- ❖ When did it happen?

- ❖ How did it start?

- ❖ How did it happen?

- ❖ Who knows about the problem?

Why is it a problem?

When you explore why it is a problem, you can better understand its level of importance and then understand why...or whether...you must address the problem with the individual you will be chaperoning. In addition to examining the problem itself, this review helps pinpoint your motivation to determine whether the problem is genuine. Ask the following questions to begin:

- ❖ Why is it a problem?

- ❖ Why do others think it is a problem?

- ❖ Are other people hurt?

- ❖ Is it part of a pattern?

- ❖ Why is it a problem for me?

- ❖ Why is it a problem for other people?

What am I going to do about the problem?

This is the planning and action part of the Why Sandwich. Once you have identified the problem and you understand why it is a problem, you may need to do something about it. Ask yourself the following questions to help you come up with a plan of action for eliminating your problem.

❖ What am I going to do about the problem?

❖ What can I do?

❖ How can I prevent the problem in the future?

❖ Can anyone help me?

❖ What have other people done in similar situations?

❖ Is there someone who can give me advice on this? (Treatment provider, clergy…?)

Assignment: Planning to Tackle Problems

1. Work with the individual you will be chaperoning to detail a list of potential problems that may arise during your chaperoning engagement. Here are some thought starters: resentment, closed channel, and power play.

2. Share your list with the treatment provider in a therapy session. Ask the treatment provider to help you and the individual you will be chaperoning select a problem and practice using the Why Sandwich to solve it.

3. Collaborate with the individual you will be chaperoning to use the Why Sandwich to solve each of the problems on your list. Ask for help from the treatment provider if you get stuck and can't solve a problem.

Things You Should Talk About

If the chaperon process is going to be successful, it will be because you and the individual you chaperon are talking about things critical to the chaperon process. Below is a list of things for the two of you to discuss:

❖ **Stress (Triggers)**: Talk with the individual you will be chaperoning about the stresses in his or her life and what initially triggers the thoughts of sexual misconduct. The more you know about what starts the downward spiral, the better you will be able to help the individual effectively use coping skills to deter the behavior.

❖ **High-Risk Situations:** Anytime the one you are chaperoning comes in contact with a high-risk person, place, or thing, you need to talk about that high-risk situation.

❖ **Grooming:** Discuss any behavior that you think might be grooming, or setup, behavior, e.g., isolating a potential victim, special relationship with a potential victim, unmonitored Internet use, and so on.

❖ **Manipulation:** Don't be surprised if the individual you are chaperoning tries to get you to violate rules or guidelines. You can still care about him or her and stick to the safety guidelines. View any attempt to get around rules as manipulation and let the treatment provider know about it. You and the treatment provider can then discuss the possible manipulation with the person you are chaperoning.

❖ **Divide and Conquer:** Perhaps the worst thing that could happen to you as a chaperon is for the individual you are chaperoning to make you feel as if you have to choose between treatment and him or her. Any time the individual makes you feel as if you have to make this choice, you are being manipulated. Actually, you are a victim of the age-old strategy of "*Divide and Conquer.*" In this case, the one you are chaperoning is trying to drive a wedge between you and the treatment provider. Once he or she has separated you and the treatment provider, it is easier for the individual to slip back into a pattern of sexual misconduct.

The nice thing about being a concerned family member or friend is that you care about what happens to the individual you are chaperoning. So, you are probably already accustomed to talking to him or her. The only thing different about being a chaperon is that you may have to talk about more challenging topics. Don't worry about saying the right thing. If you approach the conversation with a caring attitude, you can talk about anything, especially the important things.

Face it honestly. Deal with it courageously. Overcome it successfully.

Try to deal with the difficult topics now. While the one you are chaperoning is still in treatment, you have the opportunity to get feedback from the treatment provider about how to talk about and deal with the tough issues. Get practice discussing these things now so that, in the future, you can be the support system the individual you are chaperoning needs.

Assessment: How Open is Your Communication?

1. How do you feel about talking with the one you will be chaperoning about tough issues?

2. What is the worst that could happen if you talk to the person you will be chaperoning one about one of these issues?

3. What is the worst that could happen if do <u>not</u> talk to the one you will be chaperoning about one of these issues?

Weekly Chaperon Diary

When you and the individual you will be chaperoning use the Chaperon Diary, it is important to focus on the successes, as well as the challenges. This allows both of you to objectively review the individual's progress.

The Chaperon Diary allows you and the person you will be chaperoning to track successes and challenges when dealing with high-risk situations. You and the individual can complete the Chaperon Diary together. It is a good way to ensure that the two of you continue talking about the important things, such as high-risk situations and coping skills.

How you use the Chaperon Diary now will set the tone for the how you and the one you will chaperon discuss important topics long after treatment is over. Here are a few things you can do to make your conversations more effective:

1. **Communicate openly.** Talk about anything and everything that seems relevant.

2. **Avoid being defensive.** Focus on the issues not the person.

3. **Be courageous.** Face the big, hairy topics head-on. Often, those are the ones that really matter.

4. **Ask for help.** Get input from the treatment provider for challenges you can't overcome. You and the person you are chaperoning are inevitably going to have problems.

5. **Look at problems as opportunities for improvement.** It's not those who fall down who fail, but those who stay down.

Weekly Chaperon Diary: Make a diary entry every time you and the individual you chaperon have a discussion about treatment, stress, the chaperon process, or anything important. List the things you and the one you chaperon achieved. Take credit for your successes. Also describe problems, especially lingering problems. For unresolved problems, you may want to use the Why Sandwich and document the solutions you generated. Bring your Chaperon Diary to your sessions with the treatment provider.

Constant Companion

One of the duties of a chaperon is to be a constant companion to the individual you are chaperoning. Whenever the individual is in a high-risk situation, you must be within comfortable sight and sound of each other. This means that you are able to see each other clearly and talk to each other without yelling.

For example, if you and the individual go to the mall, you should be within an arms distance (about two feet) from each other. It is not OK for you to be in one store while the individual is in another. The same is true when the individual and a potential victim are at home. You should not be in the kitchen getting something to eat, while the person you are chaperoning is in the bedroom reading a book. You must stay within sight and sound of each other or that book could be replaced by something much more dangerous.

There are two major problems that pop up when trying to be a constant companion: carelessness and rejection.

Carelessness: It is possible to lose track of the individual and get separated for a moment or two. This could be an accident but you have to look at the possibility that it was the individual's plan to break free from chaperoning. He or she may be testing the waters or actually trying to begin using a sexual behavior problem.

The individual you will be chaperoning has the primary responsibility for ensuring that you are constant companions. If you become separated, it means the individual has not met an obligation of the treatment program.

On the other hand, if you are the reason for frequently losing track of the individual, it may mean you have become tired of being a chaperon. Don't be surprised if this happens. Being a chaperon is difficult. If you're unable to continue as an effective chaperon, you may want to let the treatment provider know. Keep in mind that you can take a break from chaperoning and then resume the chaperon role later. There may be others who can chaperon and take the load of you.

Frequent carelessness is a serious problem, no matter who is the cause. If you notice carelessness creeping into your chaperon experience, you and the individual must discuss it with the treatment provider.

Rejection: Once the person you will chaperon starts using the Chaperon Contract, he or she may get tired of having you (or anyone) as a constant companion. The individual may feel that he or she is being watched every minute and has no privacy or personal time. As a result, the resentment may be transferred onto you. The individual could use these feelings as a justification to reject being chaperoned and reject you as a chaperon.

Even though there are different ways to fail as a constant companion, there is really only one solution. If you and the individual encounter serious problems and frequently fail to be constant companions, the chaperon contract needs to be suspended. While it is suspended, you can work on the problem that caused it to be suspended with the treatment provider.

While the chaperon contract is suspended, you and the individual have the breathing room to work on the problems that caused the suspension. Actually, sometimes all that is needed is for you to get a break from chaperon duties for a while and return to your role as a chaperon with renewed energy and commitment.

Assessment: Your Companionship Skills

Are you a good companion? Use the definition of companion from the earlier lessons to answer these questions.

1. How is the role of chaperon different from your current relationship with the individual?

2. What impact do you think your role as chaperon will have on your relationship with the individual you will be chaperoning?

3. Do you feel comfortable communicating openly with the individual's treatment provider?

4. If you become a chaperon for this individual, how will that help him or her?

5. What impact will your role as chaperon have on you?

Assignment: Artful Dodger

1. Identify at least three times that you and the individual may fail to keep within sight and sound of each other. For each situation, explain what happened. Identify the reason it happened.

2. Pretend that the individual wants to escape being your constant companion. List 5 things the individual could do to escape being chaperoned.

3. For the 5 ways of escaping companionship listed above, provide a solution, or way to prevent it. (Once you have assumed companion duties, you and the individual should work together on coming up with solutions.)

Watch Out for Splitting

Splitting is anything that the individual you will be chaperoning does to split you from having contact, or a good relationship, with the treatment provider. When a person with a sexual behavior problem splits, the individual drives a wedge between the chaperon and the treatment provider so the person no longer has a unified team. A team divided is more easily manipulated.

When an individual tries to split a chaperon and the treatment provider, it often begins with the person being chaperoned asking the chaperon to keep a small secret. For example, let's say you discover that the one you have been chaperoning has been looking at cable TV movies for the purpose of seeing nudity. You know they have a problem with pornography and you suspect that they have just switched from Internet porn to "legitimate" movies as a means of viewing nudity. The individual might say, *"It was an accident. I had no idea the movie had so much sex. It only happened once. I promise I won't do it again. Please don't tell my treatment provider."*

In the scenario above, the truth will most likely come out anyway. Most treatment programs use annual polygraph exams. If the individual looked at sexual images once or a thousand times, it would come out during the polygraph process.

The request to lie may be for something that seems even more trivial. You may even find yourself saying something like, *"Oh, it was only a one-time deal. Besides, if it is on cable TV it is not X-rated. I don't want him (or her) to get into trouble with the treatment provider."*

Splitting generally starts with a small secret, but that's not where it stops. Shortly after keeping the first secret, you may begin to slide down the slippery slope and keep another secret…and another. One day, you will notice that what started as a grain of sand has escalated into a mountain and some of the secrets you are keeping are about major rule violations. The person you are chaperoning has successfully split you and the treatment provider. As a result, failure and more victims may be on the horizon.

Keeping secrets is not the only tool for splitting. Sometimes an individual may use guilt or threats. A common use of guilt goes something like this, *"If you tell the treatment provider I saw nudity on TV, he will send me to prison."* Other individuals might threaten, *"If you tell the treatment provider I saw nudity on TV, I might as well kill myself. First, I'm going to get drunk and then I'm just going to shoot myself."*

If the person you will be chaperoning breaks a rule, the individual has one problem. If he or she breaks a rule and keeps a secret, there are two problems: the rule violation and the secret. If an individual breaks a rule, keeps it a secret, and gets the chaperon to keep a secret, the person now has three problems. By enabling the person you are chaperoning you are only making their successful treatment more challenging.

As a chaperon, there is never a good reason to lie to the treatment provider or omit relevant information. If you are unsure whether the information is important, mention it anyway.

Assignment: A Closer Look at Splitting

1. What is splitting?

2. List 5 things you think the individual you will be chaperoning could do to split you from the treatment provider.

3. Come up with a solution to each of the five things you listed in #2. You can have the one you are chaperoning help you come up with solutions.

Ever After

Being a chaperon involves commitment and hard work. But it is also a tremendous opportunity to form an intense, lasting bond with the person you will be chaperoning. In performing the duties of a chaperon, you will be doing a great service to the person you will be chaperoning. From this service, you will also be given the gift of understanding yourself on a much deeper and more profound level.

You are doing a generous thing both for the person you will be chaperoning and for yourself. Once your work together has been successful, the two of you will have made the world a better place by helping the individual you have chaperoned to have **No New Victims!**